DRUGS & CONSEQUENCES™

THE TRUTH ABOUT PRESCRIPTION DRUGS

BASIA LEONARD and JEREMY ROBERTS

ROSEN PUBLISHING
New York

Published in 2012 by The Rosen Publishing Group, Inc.
29 East 21st Street, New York, NY 10010

First Edition

Library of Congress Cataloging-in-Publication Data

Leonard, Basia.
The truth about prescription drugs/Basia Leonard, Jeremy Roberts.—
1st ed.
p. cm.—(Drugs & consequences)
Includes bibliographical references and index.
ISBN 978-1-4488-4642-9 (library binding) 1. Drug abuse—Juvenile literature. 2. Drugs—Health aspects—Juvenile literature. 3. Substance abuse—Psychological aspects—Juvenile literature. 4. Substance abuse—Physiological aspects—Juvenile literature. I. Roberts, Jeremy, 1956– II. Title.
RC564.3.L466 2012
362.29—dc22

2011000275

Manufactured in the United States of America

CPSIA Compliance Information: Batch #S11YA: For further information, contact Rosen Publishing, New York, New York, at 1-800-237-9932.

CONTENTS

INTRODUCTION

Every year, millions of people in America abuse prescription drugs. They do this in one of several ways. They may fail to follow the directions that come with a prescription and take incorrect dosages. They may take a drug when they no longer need it. Or, they may take a drug that hasn't been prescribed for them.

In some cases, a person takes too large a dose or combines a drug with another potentially dangerous substance, such as alcohol. In other cases, a person might start taking a prescription drug for a legitimate reason and then continue to take it long after the original medical problem goes away. To get more of a drug, a person might pretend to be hurt or sick long after there is any real need for medication. Or, he or she might buy the drug from a friend.

Sometimes a drug abuser has no idea what drug he or she is taking. Little or nothing is known about the drug's side effects or how it may interact with other drugs. Some people call this recreational drug use. Others say it is just playing Russian roulette with pills. Taking a pill when you don't know what it is or where it came from is foolish. Taking medicine that hasn't been prescribed for you can end your life.

The number of teens abusing prescription drugs has been growing. Although these drugs often come from the family home and not the street, using them improperly is illegal and dangerous.

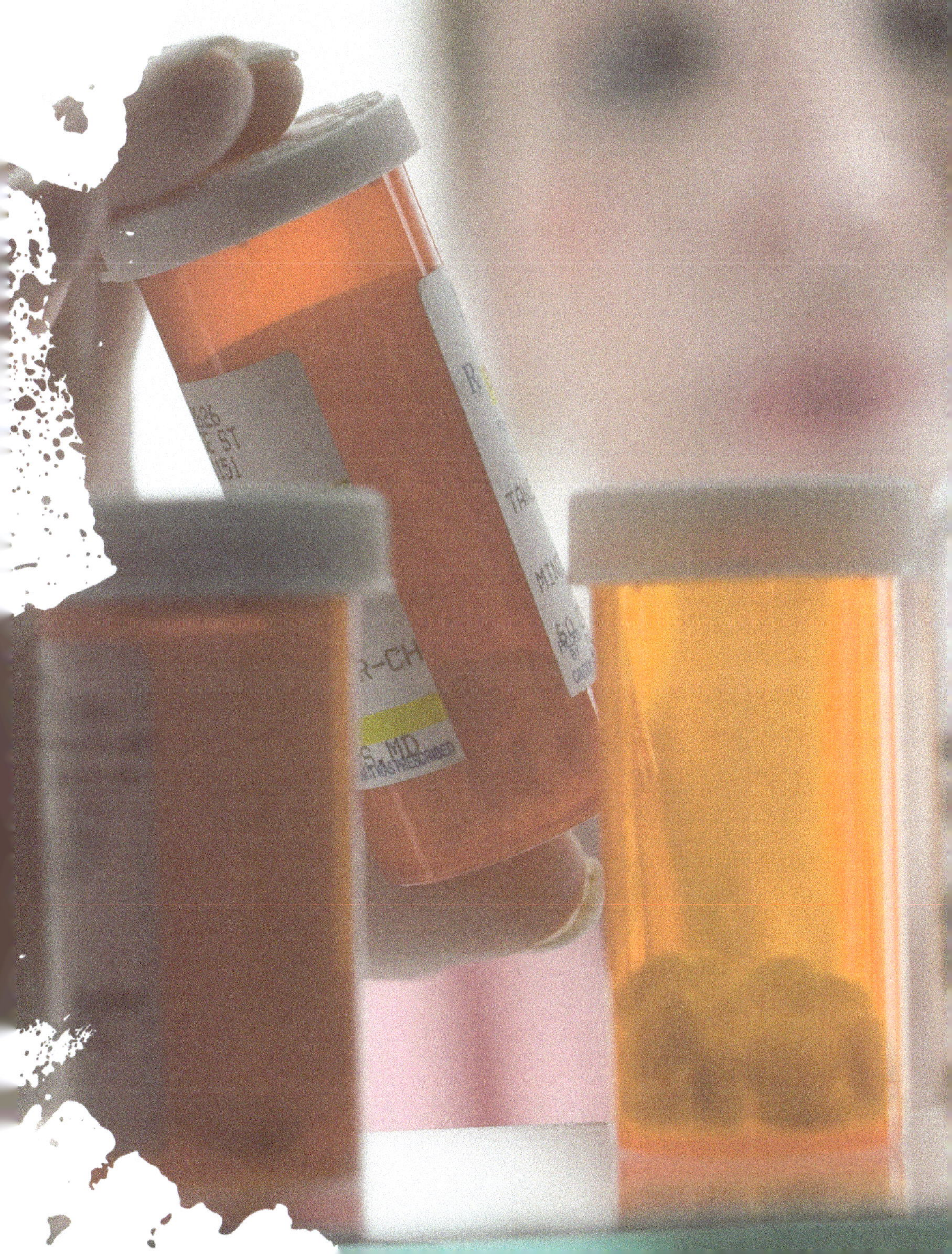

Unfortunately, a growing number of teens are abusing prescription drugs. According to a 2006 survey by Partnership for a Drug-Free America (now the Partnership at Drugfree.org), 19 percent of teens—almost one in five—have used prescription drugs for the purpose of getting high.

In this book, you will learn about different kinds of prescription drugs and the health problems they may cause if taken incorrectly or without a medical reason. You will learn about negative drug reactions and side effects. In addition, you will find resources to seek help for yourself or a friend who is dealing with chemical dependency. Most of all, you will discover that just because prescription drugs are used medically, they are not necessarily safe.

CHAPTER 1

DANGEROUS MEDICINE

Prescription drug abuse has been a problem for as long as there have been prescriptions. Certain drugs have a lengthy history of being abused. The abuse of Valium, a tranquilizer, was so widespread when your grandparents were young that a famous rock group, the Rolling Stones, wrote a song about it called "Mother's Little Helper." The song is about the growing number of ordinary, respectable women who had come to depend on pills to control their moods and deal with the stresses of life.

What's the Problem with Prescription Drugs?

Some prescription drugs have psychoactive, or mind-altering, effects, and they can be addictive. Even those drugs that are not addictive can cause problems, since their effects on the body are often complicated.

Intimate knowledge of a person's health history is important in prescribing drugs. The size and timing of dosages can be critically important and must be adjusted for the individual. Also, some drugs can have severe side effects for a small percentage of people. For example, taking certain medications can be dangerous for people with high blood pressure or heart conditions. These factors all must be weighed when prescribing drugs. The knowledge and precautions taken by the doctor and pharmacist may save a patient's life. Someone who abuses a prescription drug is ignoring these precautions and may pay for it with his or her health or life.

Of course, the potential dangers of prescription drugs shouldn't frighten you to the point that you never take any medicine. However, it is important to give doctors and pharmacists as much information as you can about any health problems, allergies, and past reactions to medicines. You should also inform your doctor of any medicines—either prescription or over-the-counter drugs—that you are currently taking. Two or more drugs can interact to create unwanted side effects.

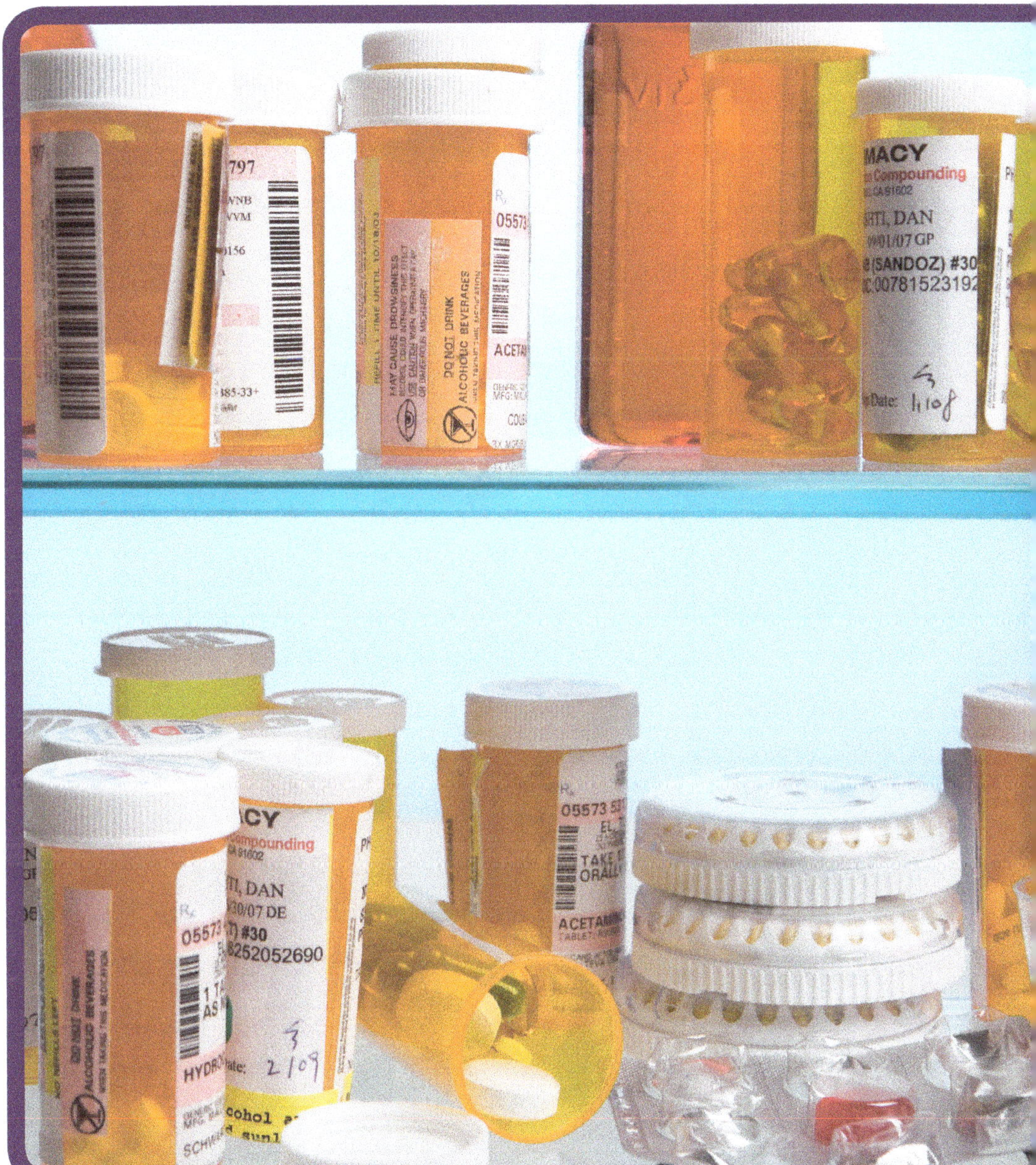

The typical medicine cabinet in a North American home contains an array of drugs. Modern medicines can improve many health conditions, but they can also cause harm if used incorrectly.

Don't be afraid to ask your doctor questions about a prescription drug and its side effects. Never take medicine that has been prescribed for someone else, even if you think you have the same illness.

Categories of Drugs

In the United States, pharmaceuticals (medicines) are divided into two main categories: over-the-counter (OTC) drugs and prescription drugs. Over-the-counter drugs can be bought almost anywhere by anyone. They include everyday drugs, such as cough medicines and antacids. In general, prescription drugs are stronger and carry more risks than over-the-counter drugs. As a result, U.S. law requires customers to have a prescription from a health-care professional in order to buy them.

In addition, some drugs in the United States are considered controlled substances. These drugs are the most highly regulated. Some drugs in this category, such as heroin, are illegal street drugs that can never be prescribed in the United States. Other drugs in this category can be prescribed in a limited and carefully controlled way.

Over-the-Counter (OTC) Drugs

Over-the-counter drugs are purchased in a store without a prescription. For the most part, they are common medicines that everyone knows about. Aspirin, cough medicine, and many antihistamines used for allergies and colds are examples of OTC

The Importance of Pharmacists

Pharmacists are trained and licensed to distribute prescription drugs. In the old days, pharmacists often mixed chemicals and made certain drugs themselves. In Great Britain, they are still called chemists. Although today's pharmacists do know a great deal about chemistry, most drugs come from manufacturers already prepared in large batches, which must be individually packaged by pharmacists and their assistants.

Pharmacists receive extensive training in many aspects of drug therapy. One of the most important things pharmacists do is check the ways in which different drugs interact. These interactions can be quite confusing, and many pharmacies use computers to help them watch for potential problems. Pharmacists also counsel patients about how to take medicines correctly and what to expect while taking them. New drugs are developed every year, and new information is gathered about existing drugs. Pharmacists must work hard to keep themselves up-to-date in their rapidly changing field.

Pharmacists are trained to provide information about drugs. When you get a new medication, ask the pharmacist questions in the store or on the phone.

medicines. Over-the-counter medicines include pills that you swallow, like the pain reliever ibuprofen. They also include drugs that you apply topically to your body, such as first-aid cream or calamine lotion. The U.S. Food and Drug Administration (FDA) estimates there are more than three hundred thousand OTC products available; new versions come out every day.

Some medicines start out as prescription drugs and then become over-the-counter drugs. Often, that happens to a drug after it has been used for many years and has shown a good record for safety and effectiveness. In most cases, medical authorities have come to understand that the drug is not easily abused. Drugs that help reduce stomach acid and relieve ulcers are examples of medicines that began as prescription drugs and then became available over the counter.

Over-the-counter drugs are usually less expensive than prescription drugs. They are easier to obtain, since you don't have to see a doctor to buy them and you don't need a pharmacist to prepare them. However, it is important to remember that over-the-counter drugs can be abused just as prescription drugs can. Even though they are generally weaker and less dangerous than prescription medicines, they still can do harm under the wrong circumstances. For example, even a small dose of aspirin irritates some people's stomachs. Taking too much aspirin can cause bleeding.

In order to be safe, it is important to read the labels on OTC drugs, since they contain information about the drugs' uses, ingredients, warnings, and directions. Follow the directions

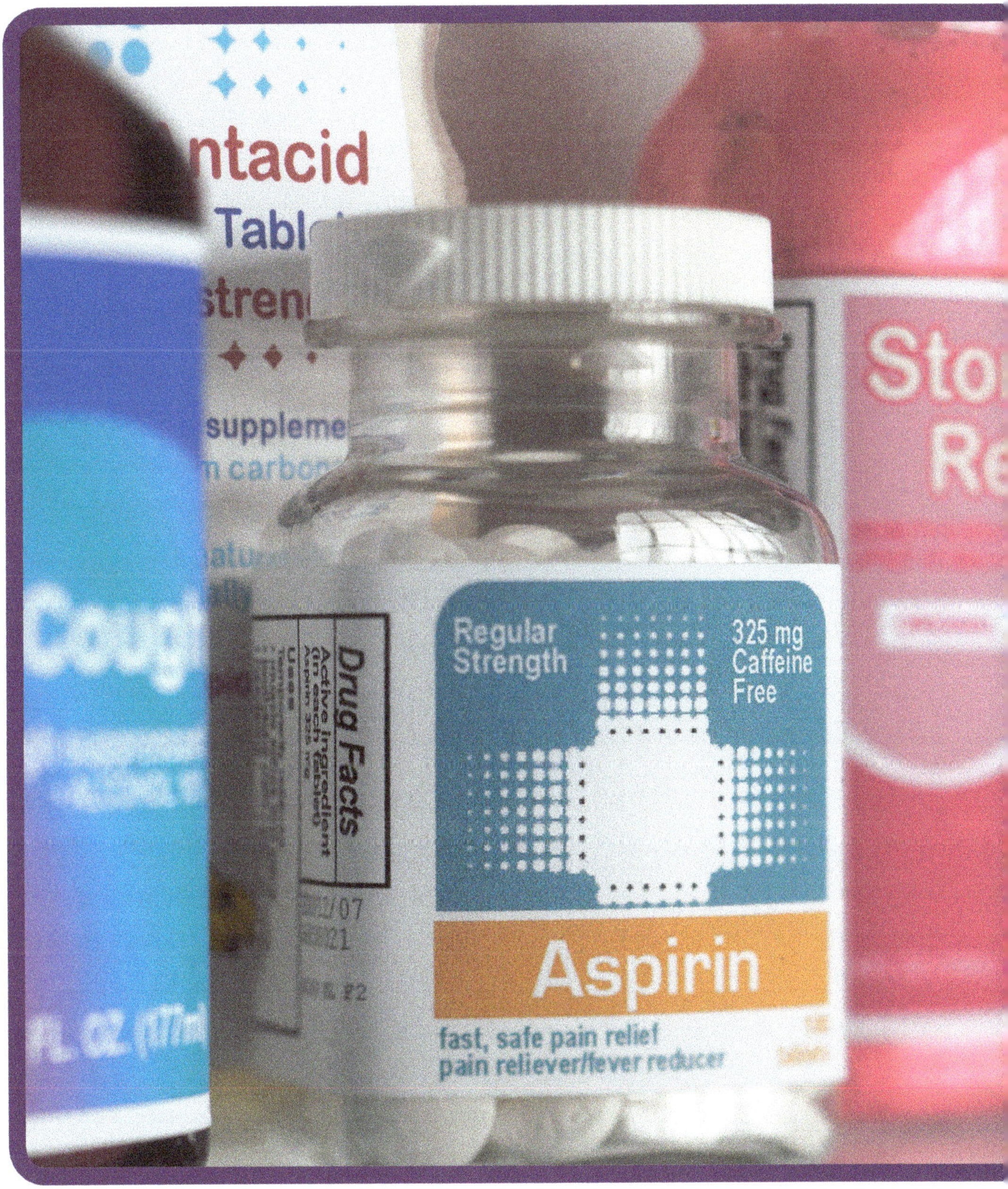

OTC drugs enable people to relieve many annoying symptoms. However, safe use of these products requires knowledge and care, as any drug can cause adverse effects.

on all OTC medicines carefully. Since new information becomes known all the time, individuals should read labels even when using a drug they have taken in the past. Also, drugs with the same brand name may contain different ingredients, since many OTC drugs have a variety of formulations. Customers with questions about OTC drugs can ask a pharmacist for help.

Prescription Drugs

Prescription drugs are purchased in a pharmacy and require a medical prescription written for a particular patient. In most cases, a doctor must personally examine the patient and conclude that a certain drug will help the patient's condition before writing the prescription. The prescription for the drug is then given to a licensed pharmacist, who makes sure that the right drug and the proper dosage are prepared. Ultimately, it is up to the patient to follow directions and take the medicine correctly. Federal and state laws control prescription drugs. These laws dictate how such drugs can be prescribed, sold, and used.

A drug's potential to be abused or to cause addiction is one reason why it may be available only by prescription. However, that is not the only reason. Many drugs are not addictive, but they may have strong side effects or cause serious problems for

Drug warning label stickers on prescription containers highlight the most important instructions for safe use of a medication.

some people when used incorrectly. Powerful medicines, such as antibiotics, must be chosen carefully to do the most good and the least harm. In some cases, a drug may be so new that doctors are still learning how best to use it.

In all of these cases, the prescription system allows doctors and other health-care workers to keep an eye on things. The system is designed to protect patients, who may not have detailed knowledge about a drug or who may be vulnerable to the medicine's side effects. If patients take a drug under a doctor's care, they can contact the doctor immediately if they experience problems. The doctor can change the dosage or the drug if necessary.

Unfortunately, in a small percentage of cases, doctors and pharmacists are part of the problem. For example, some doctors may not check a patient as carefully as they should to make sure that a certain drug is actually needed. Some doctors may not monitor patients carefully while they are taking prescription drugs. A small number of unethical doctors may write prescriptions even though they know or suspect that the medicine will be abused.

Controlled Substances

Drugs that have a high potential for abuse are under special regulation by the federal government. They are called controlled substances. The Controlled Substances Act (CSA) states the law for different classifications of drugs. The law places drugs into five different lists, called schedules, based on their

A Wise Decision

The dentist gave Matt a shake of his head. "I'm afraid that tooth is going to have to come out," he said.

"Will it hurt?" asked Matt. His mouth ached so badly that the words slurred together and he practically choked getting them out.

"Well, it won't hurt as much in the long run if we take care of it now," said the dentist. "We can dull the pain during the surgery with Novocain and laughing gas. And I'll give you a prescription for some Empirin with codeine. That will make it feel better."

Matt was dubious. But sure enough, the Novocain and laughing gas dulled the pain. His head felt very light. His sister had come with him to the dentist. They stopped at the drugstore on the way home. The pharmacist explained that Empirin with codeine was a combination of aspirin and codeine. The aspirin helped relieve pain and inflammation, or swelling. Codeine was a pain reliever. The two drugs worked very well together, the pharmacist explained.

Matt agreed, especially when he felt better shortly after he took his prescribed pill. In fact, he thought he felt calmer and more at ease when he took the drug. He certainly slept very well.

On Thursday, he took his last pill. Though he no longer felt any pain, Matt thought about calling the dentist and asking for more pills.

"They made me feel more relaxed," he explained. "But then I read the paper that the pharmacist gave me. It told all about the drug. There were all sorts of possible side effects. Then I saw that it could be addictive. I decided that I didn't want to mess with it."

medical usefulness and potential for abuse. These schedules rank drugs from one to five, based on how harmful they can be. Officials at the U.S. Drug Enforcement Administration (DEA) help carry out and enforce the law.

According to federal law, schedule I drugs are drugs that have no currently accepted medical use. They are not considered safe for anyone to use, and doctors cannot prescribe them. This category includes illegal substances, such as heroin.

Schedule II drugs do have legitimate medical uses, but they can be easily abused. Using them improperly can be catastrophic. Abuse of these drugs can lead to severe psychological or physical dependence. This category includes opium and morphine. Once prescribed, schedule II drugs cannot be refilled without going to the doctor and getting a new prescription.

Drugs in schedules III, IV, and V have legitimate medical uses and are less addictive and dangerous than drugs in schedules I and II. However, they, too, can be abused. Refills of these drugs are limited.

It is likely that you or someone you know has taken a drug in schedules III–V. For example, aspirin with codeine, a schedule III drug, is often given after oral surgery. The combination of codeine and aspirin is a very effective painkiller, if used correctly. Because the drug can be abused and lead to dependence, however, it is categorized as schedule III. Dependence means that the body adjusts to taking the drug so that the person cannot function normally without it.

By looking at the drug schedules, one can see that some prescription drugs and illegal drugs share similar properties and potential for abuse. Using prescription drugs to get high can lead to dependence and addiction, just as using heroin can.

CHAPTER 2

PRESCRIPTION FOR ABUSE: NARCOTICS AND DEPRESSANTS

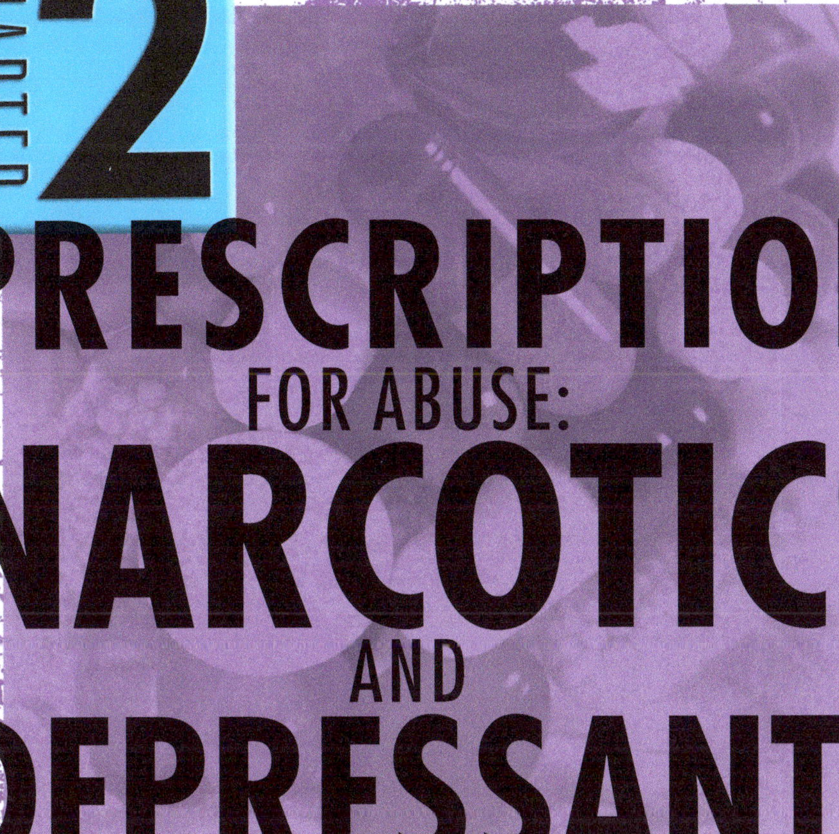

Prescription drugs are of vital importance to many people. Painkillers, for example, make surgery possible. Prescription drugs can help people overcome difficult physical and mental problems. However, they also can be very dangerous, especially when they are abused. And some can be very tempting. Eight of the top thirteen drugs abused by high school seniors are prescription drugs and OTC medicines, according to the 2009 Monitoring the Future study from the University of Michigan's Institute for Social Research.

A Brush with Death

Alyssa rubbed her face and glanced toward the front of the classroom. Her math teacher, Mr. Morrison, was explaining how to solve a geometry problem. Math was one of her best subjects, but suddenly nothing Mr. Morrison was saying made sense. In fact, it sounded to Alyssa as if he were speaking a foreign language. She felt incredibly tired. She closed her eyes and felt herself slipping from her chair. Then she hit the floor.

The next thing Alyssa knew, the school nurse was there, along with the vice principal. She felt very far away, as if she were lying at the bottom of a ten-foot-deep pool. The nurse, normally a calm lady, was screaming. She shouted, "Her skin looks blue! Call 9-1-1!"

Two emergency medical technicians came into the room. There were questions. Had she taken any medications? Alyssa tried to tell them that she had taken two pills. They were prescription pills that her friend Paige had given her. It was a prescription that Paige's mom had gotten some time ago—painkillers or something. Alyssa had even taken one once before. But she was so dizzy and tired that her mouth just didn't seem to work.

Alyssa had taken two pills of Percocet, a powerful pain reliever containing oxycodone and acetaminophen. Ordinarily this painkiller can alleviate suffering and is very useful when prescribed properly. But in improper doses, it can cause death.

Alyssa's story had a happy ending. She didn't stop breathing or have a seizure. Alyssa ended up having her stomach pumped, which wasn't very pleasant. A tube was inserted through her mouth, down the esophagus (food pipe), and into the stomach. Her stomach contents were removed using suction to get rid of the overdosed medication. After she recovered, she had to explain to her parents what had happened, and she and Paige were suspended from the field hockey team. Paige was taken to family court and nearly charged with a crime. But considering what could have happened, everyone involved was very lucky.

Frequently abused prescription drugs can be divided into a number of major classes. Narcotic painkillers and depressants are two major classes of prescription drugs abused by teens and adults.

Narcotic Painkillers

Narcotics are drugs that belong to the opiate/opioid family. Drugs in this group are powerful painkillers that are designed to relieve extreme pain. All are chemically related or are chemically similar to opium, which comes from poppies and has a long history as an addictive drug. The drugs are divided into two groups, according to how they are made. Opiates come from nature, that is, from the juice of the poppy plant. Opioids are made synthetically in the laboratory.

Commonly abused members of this drug family include the opioids hydrocodone and oxycodone. These powerful painkillers are used to treat mild to severe pain in patients who have had surgery or who suffer from painful conditions. These drugs are often combined with nonnarcotic painkillers like aspirin or acetaminophen. Hydrocodone combinations are among the most prescribed drugs in the country. Common brand names include Vicodin and Lortab. Oxycodone products, including OxyContin, Percodan, and Percocet, are also widely prescribed by doctors. Other abused opioids include Demerol (meperidine) and Dilaudid (hydromorphone).

Narcotic painkillers can cause euphoria, drowsiness, and slowed breathing. An overdose of these powerful drugs can result in convulsions, coma, or death.

All of these opioids are schedule II drugs, which means they carry a high risk of physical and psychological dependence. Unfortunately, according to the 2009 Monitoring the Future study, 9.2 percent of twelfth graders reported taking narcotic painkillers without a prescription during the previous year.

Another member of the narcotics family is heroin, an illegal schedule I drug. An extremely addictive and destructive drug, heroin is the most infamous member of the opiates. Some narcotics are stronger than others, but when used improperly, all members of this drug family can be habit forming.

Some people who take narcotics have an initial feeling of euphoria. Then they sink into a kind of gentle oblivion, in which they cannot feel much pain—just the sort of thing patients need when undergoing or recovering from surgery. In general, these drugs slow breathing and other bodily functions. The effects of such drugs can be magnified if combined with a depressant, such as alcohol.

An overdose of a narcotic drug can cause life-threatening breathing complications, convulsions, coma, or death. Respiratory complications can occur from taking just one large dose or mixing a narcotic with alcohol or other drugs that slow breathing. Further, users develop a tolerance to these drugs quickly. This means that over time, it takes more and more of the drug to produce the same pain relief or rush. Abusers rapidly reach the point where they are taking dangerously high doses. According to the Centers for Disease Control and

Mixing prescription drugs or taking a large dose of one drug can result in death. Talented artists who have been lost to prescription drug overdoses include Heath Ledger (*above*, as the Joker), Michael Jackson, and Elvis Presley.

Prevention (CDC), opioid painkillers are a leading cause of drug overdose deaths.

People who use a narcotic for several weeks or more may develop a physical dependence on the drug. This means that they must keep taking the drug in order to avoid withdrawal

symptoms. Some withdrawal symptoms that users or abusers can experience include diarrhea, vomiting, pain, cold flashes, insomnia, and restlessness. To prevent patients from developing tolerance and dependence, doctors usually prescribe narcotics only for short periods of time. They also supervise patients when stopping use to prevent or reduce withdrawal symptoms.

Depressants

Depressants are a class of drugs that slow down, or depress, the activity of the central nervous system. These drugs can be very helpful for people with health conditions such as anxiety and panic attacks, sleep disorders, and seizure disorders.

When used appropriately under a doctor's care, depressants reduce tension and nervousness and promote a relaxed, calm mental state. They are also used to relax muscles and bring on sleep. As a result, they are often referred to as tranquilizers or sedatives. When given in high doses, depressants can be used as anesthesia. Because they can have an intoxicating

Unhappy teens may be tempted to try a drug to change how they feel. Don't take a drug unless a doctor prescribes it to treat your medical or psychological condition.

effect, depressants have the potential for abuse. Alcohol and other drugs can multiply their effects.

One of the best-known depressants is Valium (diazepam). It belongs to a family of drugs called benzodiazepines, which are used to treat anxiety. Other drugs in this family include Ativan (lorazepam), Halcion (triazolam), and Xanax (alprazolam). These drugs depress the body's natural reactions, such as fear and nervousness. When used in combination with psychological counseling, they are effective weapons against anxiety and panic disorders. In some situations, they can help patients who need to get sleep or who need to recover from traumatic situations.

However, Valium and its kin can be abused. When used incorrectly, benzodiazepines, or "benzos," can cause physical dependence and addiction. A person with an addiction seeks out a drug compulsively. He or she continues to use the drug despite negative personal consequences and harmful health effects. According to the 2009 Monitoring the Future survey, 6.3 percent of high school seniors reported abusing tranquilizers such as Valium and Xanax within the previous year.

Barbiturates are another family of depressant drugs. All barbiturates are man-made. The drugs were invented in the 1860s and first used in medical practice in 1903. In the past, barbiturates were prescribed for anxiety disorders and sleeplessness, but they were found to be highly addictive. As a result, newer drugs have largely replaced them in treating these conditions. However, doctors still use barbiturates to treat some forms of epilepsy. Examples of barbiturates are Amytal (amobarbital),

Club Drugs

Two depressant drugs that have gained a very bad reputation are Rohypnol and GHB. These drugs tend to be abused at nightclubs, bars, raves, trances, or other party scenes.

Rohypnol (flunitrazepam), known on the street as "roofies," is a member of the benzodiazepine family. The drug is chemically similar to Valium or Xanax. Rohypnol is known as a "date rape" drug because some people have used the drug to render others unconscious and rape them. It can easily be added to drinks, where it dissolves. Because the drug acts as a sedative, someone taking it may pass out or become more open to suggestion than under normal circumstances. While Rohypnol is prescribed as a sleep medication or sedative in some other countries, it is not manufactured or approved for medical use in the United States. Its importation is banned.

GHB, or gamma hydroxybutyrate, is a depressant drug that is used as a sedative and anesthetic in some other countries. Most forms of GHB are illegal in the United States. GHB is another one of the "date rape" drugs. It has been used to render victims unconscious and thus unable to offer testimony against their attackers. One form of GHB, with the brand name Xyrem, is approved in the United States for the treatment of narcolepsy. This is a rare condition in which people have sudden daytime sleep attacks. Abuse of GHB can cause serious medical problems, including seizures, loss of consciousness, coma, and death. It can also lead to dependence, which may include craving the drug and severe withdrawal symptoms.

GHB and Rohypnol have been used in sexual assaults of young victims that go to clubs and raves for fun.

Seconal (secobarbital), and Nembutal (sodium pentobarbital), all of which are all schedule II drugs.

Even though doctors prescribe barbiturates less frequently than in the past, people still abuse them. In the 2009 Monitoring the Future study, 5.2 percent of twelfth graders said they took barbiturates without a prescription in the previous year.

Taking depressant drugs of any kind can lead to addiction. Depressants can also lead to tolerance, so larger doses are needed to get the same initial effects. In addition, taking depressants can lead to physical dependence. Users can experience severe withdrawal symptoms when the drug is reduced or stopped. These symptoms include anxiety, insomnia, loss of appetite, and muscle tremors. If someone suddenly stops taking a depressant drug, the slowed brain activity can rebound and race out of control, resulting in seizures, delirium, or even death. Therefore, someone who wants to discontinue use of a depressant should do so with a doctor's guidance.

In addition, depressants should never be combined with alcohol, prescription pain medicines, OTC cold and allergy medications, or any other drugs that cause drowsiness. These drug combinations can slow both the heart and respiration, which can be fatal.

It's important to remember that many of these drugs can be beneficial when taken under the direction of a doctor. From patients undergoing surgery to sleep disorder sufferers, modern medicine plays an important role in improving everyone's quality of life. However, all bets are off when medicines are used incorrectly or by people who do not need them.

MYTHS & FACTS

MYTH Prescription drugs are medications, so they are safer to use than illegal street drugs.

FACT Many prescription drugs are powerful and can have adverse side effects. Hospitalizations and deaths due to prescription drug poisoning have increased greatly over the last decade. According to an article by Katherine Harmon in *Scientific American*, by 2006 overdoses of opioid painkillers alone were causing more deaths than overdoses of cocaine and heroin combined.

MYTH It is legal to use and share prescription drugs.

FACT Possessing or using a prescription medication without a doctor's prescription is illegal. Giving or selling prescription drugs to someone else—or having the "intent to distribute"—violates state and federal laws. Consequences of possession or distribution can include jail time, fines, loss of one's driver's license, court-ordered drug treatment, and other penalties.

MYTH The best way to stop taking a prescription drug is to go cold turkey.

FACT If someone who is abusing a prescription drug wants to stop, suddenly withdrawing all doses is risky. Depending on the drug involved, withdrawal symptoms can include irregular heartbeat, seizures, pain, hot flashes, nausea, vomiting, and other symptoms. Adverse emotional reactions, such as depression and anger, can also occur. Instead, the person should get help from a doctor and/or addiction specialist to taper off the medicine slowly and safely.

CHAPTER 3

GETTING AN EDGE: STIMULANTS AND STEROIDS

A high school junior is busy juggling classes, SAT preparation, and a starring role in the school play with many lines to memorize. He is having trouble managing his time and maintaining his focus. A close friend has taken medicine for attention deficit/hyperactivity disorder (ADHD) since childhood. He thinks about asking to borrow some pills to help him stay up later, study harder, and work more efficiently.

Another student is staring at himself in the mirror. He has been eating well and exercising like a demon. However, he is still not happy with the size of his muscles. He has added extra swimming laps and free weight repetitions, but he is not satisfied with his physique. He finds steroids advertised for sale on the Internet.

A growing number of young people are experimenting with prescription medicines to help them get an "edge" in academics, sports, or their social lives. They think of these drugs as ways to maximize their performance with minimal risk. According to Dr. Richard Kadison in the *New England Journal of Medicine*, this idea is reinforced by the many commercials on television telling people to "ask your doctor if this pill is right for you." People come to believe that there is a "magic bullet" that can solve their problems.

However, taking stimulants or steroids without a true medical need is unsafe. The practice can lead to dependence, addiction, and other dire health consequences.

Stimulants

Sometimes called uppers, stimulants are a category of substances that stimulate bodily activity and make people feel more alert and energetic. Stimulants range from caffeine, which is an ingredient in coffee and some sodas, to cocaine, crack, and methamphetamine. Legitimate uses of stimulants include fighting illnesses such as ADHD, narcolepsy, and some forms of depression. Some prescription stimulants, such as phentermine, are used as appetite suppressants to help people lose weight.

The most important family of medical stimulants is the amphetamine group. In general, these drugs speed up the body's activities and processes. Taking one is like feeding a steady stream of adrenaline into the bloodstream. Dextroamphetamine, the active ingredient in the drugs Adderall and Dexedrine, is used to treat ADHD.

Methylphenidate, found in the drugs Ritalin and Concerta, is another stimulant. Ritalin has become a very important drug over the past twenty years because of its use in treating ADHD. Even though it is a stimulant and patients with ADHD are hyperactive, the drug counteracts that hyperactivity. Instead of speeding up nervous activity in these patients, Ritalin slows it down. Ritalin usually acts as a stimulant for people without ADHD who take it without a prescription. After the initial rush, however, the body tends to crash sharply, that is, sink into a state of depression.

Unfortunately, the fact that these drugs are widely available for ADHD has made them easier to abuse. In some cases, patients have given their prescription pills to friends. In other cases, the drugs are stolen or illegally obtained. On college campuses, students have used these medicines as "study drugs" to try to increase alertness or stay awake while cramming for exams.

Stimulant drugs such as Ritalin can ease the symptoms of children, like this boy, who suffer from ADHD. Easy access to the drugs has increased their use for nonmedical reasons.

Abusing stimulants can be extremely dangerous. High doses can cause an increase in blood pressure and pulse rate, irregular heartbeat, dangerously high body temperatures, and the potential for heart failure or seizures. Accidental death is a possible

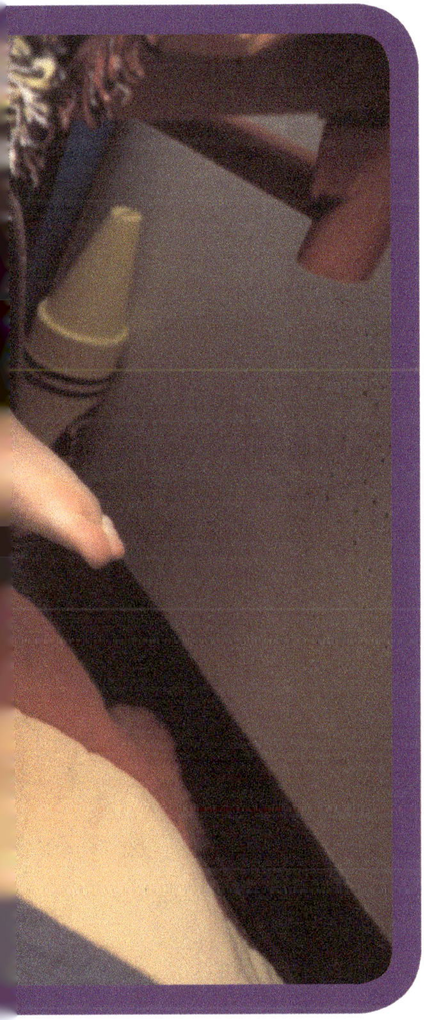

result. Physical exertion while taking stimulants, or mixing stimulants with other drugs, increases these hazards. For some people, taking high doses of certain stimulants can lead to feelings of agitation, hostility, or paranoia.

Caffeine, at least in the amounts found in coffee and soda, is generally considered harmless and is not a scheduled drug. Some studies have raised questions about consuming large amounts of caffeine, however. Many doctors now recommend moderation. In addition, in November 2010, the FDA announced that alcoholic beverages made with caffeine are unsafe. Beverages such as Four Loko, whose maker agreed to remove the caffeine, had been nicknamed "blackout in a can" by some users. The caffeine masked the effect of alcohol for many drinkers, leading them to consume much larger amounts of alcohol than they could normally tolerate. According to CNN, in October 2010, nine underage students at Central Washington University were hospitalized after drinking Four Loko, both on its own and mixed with other drinks.

Anabolic Steroids

Anabolic steroids are among the most controversial prescription drugs. Anabolic steroids are synthetic substances that are chemically similar to testosterone, the male sex hormone. The drugs promote the growth of muscle and the development of male sexual characteristics. Doctors prescribe steroids to treat delayed puberty, impotence, and diseases that cause patients to lose muscle mass, such as cancer and AIDS.

Anabolic steroids are different from many other abused drugs because they do not cause users to feel euphoric or high. Instead, athletes and others abuse anabolic steroids in an attempt to develop bigger, stronger muscles; an improved physical appearance; and enhanced sports performance. Commonly abused steroids include Anadrol (oxymetholone), Dianabol (methandrostenolone), Deca-Durabolin (nandrolone decanoate), and THG (tetrahydrogestrinone).

According to federal and state laws, it is illegal to use, possess, or sell steroids for bodybuilding and performance enhancement. Doctors will not prescribe these substances for young, healthy people. In 2004, steroidal supplements, such as "andro" (androstenedione), also became illegal in the United States. Most sports conferences routinely test for steroids. Anyone who is discovered to be using them is banned from competition. A host of organizations, including the American Medical Association (AMA), condemn their use. Congress has held hearings to determine the extent of steroid use in professional sports.

A Sad Situation

Ellen, a high school psychologist, was counseling a student when she was startled by a knock on her door. Staff members never interrupted her during a session unless there was an emergency. As soon as Ellen opened the door and saw the principal's ashen face, she knew that this was one.

Blake was an above-average student, an outstanding athlete, and a popular guy. A linebacker on the school's football team, he had been secretly using anabolic steroids to bulk up during the season. He believed that if he became bigger, faster, and stronger, he could help his team win the state championship. He also hoped to get an athletic scholarship for college. Unfortunately, Blake did not know that taking and then suddenly stopping steroids could cause severe psychological effects. After football season, he had fallen into a deep depression. Over the weekend, he had tried to commit suicide. He was in the hospital in serious condition.

The principal and Ellen discussed how to deal with the incident. The entire school was in a panic over it. Students were crying. The principal made an announcement over the loudspeaker. A lot of students seemed relieved when word came that Blake was going to be OK. But Ellen was still worried. How many times had Blake, and everyone else in school, heard about how dangerous it was to take drugs?

"It's easy to tell kids not to do it," she told her sister later. "But it's hard to say it in a way that they'll pay attention to."

In the next few weeks, Ellen and one of the school guidance counselors discussed the incident with students. They used discussions and role-playing games to help kids learn about prescription drugs and work through their feelings. Blake eventually recovered and returned to school.

Still, Ellen had questions. "How do you reach everybody?" she wondered. "How do you make people believe what you're telling them? How do you tell them that the risk isn't worth the gain?"

Why are people so concerned? Steroids build muscles; isn't that a good thing? In addition to being a method of cheating, anabolic steroids are dangerous drugs with a wide range of negative side effects. In both men and women, steroids can

Former major league pitcher Roger Clemens testified at a 2008 congressional hearing about steroid use in baseball. Trainer Brian McNamee contradicted Clemens's claim that he had never used performance-enhancing drugs.

cause liver damage, liver tumors, and liver cancer. They can increase blood pressure and cause heart attacks and strokes, even in athletes under thirty. Men who take them have an increased risk of prostate cancer. Because many steroids are injected with needles, users are at risk for contracting dangerous infections, such as HIV/AIDS and hepatitis.

Anabolic steroids can alter both men's and women's natural hormonal states, causing unwanted changes in the body. Adult men can experience acne, shrinking of the testicles, reduced sperm count, baldness, and breast development. Adult women can experience acne, increased body and facial hair, deepening of the voice, and loss of monthly periods. In adolescent boys and girls, anabolic steroids can stunt growth. The high hormone levels can prematurely signal the bones to stop growing. With continued use of steroids, some of these changes in men and women can be irreversible.

Anabolic steroids can cause negative psychological changes as well. In some people, they trigger irritability, mood swings, and aggressive behavior, known as "roid rage." When an abuser

Taking steroids can cause severe, long-lasting health consequences, especially in teens. Instead, use weight training and good nutrition as strategies to build powerful muscles.

stops taking steroids, he or she can become depressed and even suicidal.

Scientists believe that it is safest, in the long run, to improve muscles and sports performance through proper diet

and conditioning. Given the long-term hazards—not to mention the potential legal penalties—athletes are better off steering clear of steroids, no matter how tempting they may be.

OTC Cough and Cold Medicines

Prescription medicines aren't the only drugs that are abused, of course. Over-the-counter drugs can also be used incorrectly to get high.

Cough and cold medicines are among the most frequently abused over-the-counter medicines. Many of these products contain the active ingredient dextromethorphan (DXM). While safe as a cough suppressant in the recommended amount, DXM can produce a high when consumed in large amounts. Drinking large quantities of cough and cold medicines is sometimes called "dexing," "robotripping," or "robodosing." The last two slang terms refer to Robitussin, the name of a popular brand of cough medicine. However, there are numerous brands of OTC cough and cold medicines that can be abused.

Although DXM can be taken safely in small doses to suppress a cough, ingesting a large amount can sicken or even kill you.

Abusing DXM is a dangerous practice. Possible consequences of an overdose include:

- impaired judgment
- loss of coordination
- dizziness, nausea, and vomiting
- increased heart rate and blood pressure
- hot flashes or fever
- numbness
- hallucinations
- seizures
- brain damage
- death

Because OTC drugs are legal and easy to buy, many teens think they are safe no matter what. The truth is, abusing over-the-counter medicines can be just as harmful as taking prescription drugs or illegal street drugs. It can be deadly.

TEN GREAT QUESTIONS TO ASK A DOCTOR

1. What is the name of the medicine you are prescribing for me, and what is it supposed to do?

2. How and when do I take it, and for how long?

3. When should I expect the medicine to begin to work, and how will I know if it is working?

4. Are there any side effects with this drug? What are they, and what do I do if they occur?

5. What symptoms will let me know that I've taken too much or that this drug doesn't agree with me?

6. Are there any substances I should avoid while taking this drug?

7. Is there a chance of developing dependence or addiction to this drug? How do I prevent this?

8. I have a history of substance abuse in my family. Is this prescription still safe for me?

9. I've been taking a prescription drug habitually. How can I stop this drug safely?

10. What is involved in treatment for prescription drug addiction?

CHAPTER 4

STAYING SAFE

The reasons for abusing prescription drugs are often similar to the reasons for smoking or drinking. People want to feel a little different or a little better. For many teens, taking drugs is a way to show that they are grown up or that they can fit in. For others, it is a way of cutting loose. Many young people have a difficult time thinking ahead and considering the consequences of their behavior. Many teens believe there will not be any price to pay for experimenting with drugs. Some don't take prescription drug abuse as seriously as they do other forms of drug abuse. That can be a serious mistake.

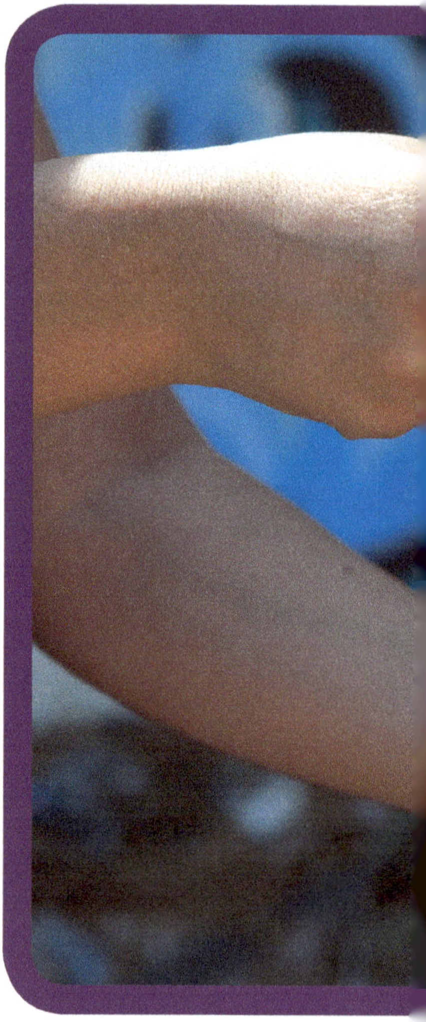

Not a Game

A teen that abuses prescription drugs may not even know what he or she is ingesting, let alone the amount in a safe dose. That is why prescription drug abuse can be just as dangerous as taking illegal street drugs. A doctor's prescription for a painkiller may be very appropriate for a 300-pound (136-kilogram) man who is laid up in bed with torn ligaments. It could prove fatal for a 90-pound (41-kg) young woman who has just consumed half a bottle of vodka.

Street or "home" versions of prescription medicines present another problem. These versions may contain impurities that multiply the drug's effects or side effects. The substances may not even be what the seller says or thinks they are. There is no quality control in the black market.

Purchasing a pharmaceutical from a dealer is especially risky, since the manufacturer and ingredients of the substance are unknown.

Reactions and Interactions

Even when used correctly, prescription drugs can prove deadly. That's because they occasionally have unforeseen effects. For example, people can experience allergic reactions to different medicines.

Allergic reactions to drugs are only one potential problem. As drugs become more chemically complex, the ways in which they interact with other substances become more complicated. Pharmacists study these drug-drug interactions. They can often prevent a patient from having trouble, but only if they know all of the drugs that a patient is taking. That is why, even if you go to the same drugstore all the time, it is a good idea to discuss all of your medications—and the possible interactions with other drugs—whenever you get a new prescription. That includes over-the-counter drugs as well. Some medicines, such as cold remedies, may contain ingredients that will react with other prescription drugs.

The most dangerous interactions often come when a drug's effects are multiplied beyond what's intended. Multiplicative effects are a special problem when drugs are abused, since there aren't any experts around to warn you of the dangers. Alcohol makes for an especially deadly mix. There have been numerous cases of people dying after mixing alcohol and barbiturates or similar pills. In effect, alcohol and drugs are a package plan for shutting down your body's vital functions.

Be an Informed Patient

Potential harmful reactions don't mean that you should be paranoid about taking medicine prescribed by your doctor.

Antibiotic Emergency

Katie and Michael were out in the backyard doing some gardening. Suddenly Michael realized that Katie wasn't in the garden anymore. He called her but didn't get an answer. Finally, he found her nearby, sitting on the ground in the shade. Katie looked frightened and her face looked red. She could barely talk. When he thought to check her pulse, he found it was very weak.

"My throat feels tight and my tongue feels thick," she said. "I'm scared."

Katie had been to the doctor earlier that day. She had been diagnosed with an internal infection and had been given a prescription for an antibiotic. She had just taken her first dose a couple of hours ago.

"Maybe we should call the doctor," said Michael. Katie was so weak, she didn't argue, which convinced Michael that something must be wrong.

The doctor told them to go to the emergency room immediately. It turned out that Katie was having an allergic reaction to the drug she was taking. Although she didn't know it at the time, she was allergic to anything containing penicillin. Katie was experiencing symptoms of anaphylaxis, a severe allergic reaction that can sometimes be fatal.

Luckily, after getting an injection of epinephrine, Katie's symptoms began to subside. Epinephrine works to relax respiratory muscles, constrict blood vessels, stimulate the heart, and reduce swelling. Katie also received further treatment with other medications to make sure the symptoms did not come back. Of course, Katie had to stop taking the drug that caused the reaction. Her doctor was able to give her a prescription for a different drug to fight her infection.

Most allergic reactions to drugs are milder than Katie's. Antibiotics such as penicillin are among the most common drugs to which people are allergic. In most cases, the reaction is simply a rash or hives. Still, doctors do not take any reactions lightly. Although it is rare, severe cases can block normal breathing and can be life threatening. Health experts say that it is important to alert doctors, dentists, and pharmacists to any allergies that you know about. If, after taking a medicine, you develop unusual or disturbing symptoms, you should immediately contact the physician who prescribed the drug.

Reactions occur in a very small percentage of cases. However, they do mean that you should be an informed patient. Your doctor and pharmacist usually know a great deal about the medicines you have been prescribed or want to buy over the counter. It is a good idea to ask these professionals many questions about your medicines. You can also get information from publications such as *The Pill Book* by Harold M. Silverman, which is published by Bantam Books and is updated every few years.

Information on different drugs is also available from Web sites and pharmaceutical companies. However, be wary of the medical information you get from Web sites unless they are sponsored by reputable medical or governmental organizations. The U.S. National Library of Medicine (NLM) maintains a Web site called MedlinePlus (http://www.nlm.nih.gov/medlineplus) that provides authoritative health information, including information on many prescription and OTC drugs.

When taking any needed medication, it's important to follow all directions that come with the medicine. Unless the instructions say otherwise, prescriptions should be taken until they are gone. Always alert your doctor or your pharmacist if you experience a reaction to a drug, or even if you think you might be experiencing a reaction. Never combine drugs without your doctor's knowledge. Above all, don't mix alcohol or illegal substances with prescription drugs.

Knowing your health history, your doctor can discuss whether a drug's potential benefits outweigh the risks.

If Someone You Know Has a Problem

Prescription drug abuse is a serious problem in the United States. Strategies for dealing with it vary, depending on the situation and the drug involved. Many programs are similar to those used to combat other types of substance abuse.

If you suspect that you or someone you know has a problem with prescription drugs, try to get help as soon as you can.

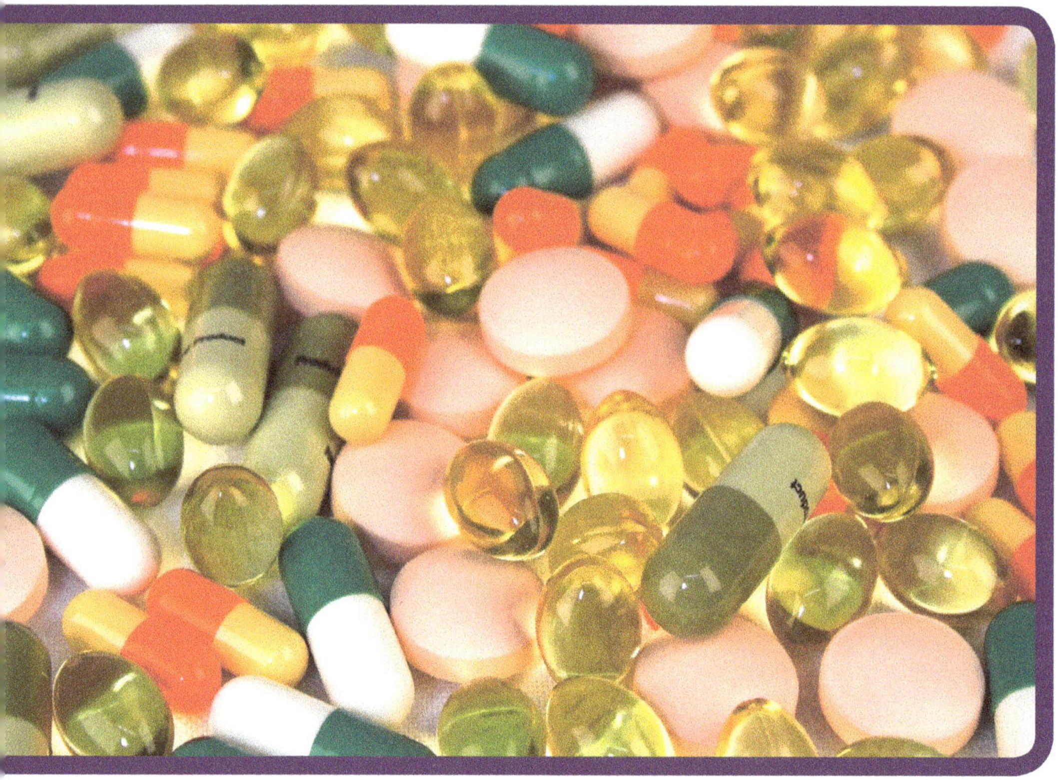

There are thousands of medications out there, and they need to be handled with care. Make the choice not to gamble with your future.

Guidance departments and school nurses may offer help and advice. They are often in touch with local substance abuse assistance programs. Other sources of help include doctors, mental health organizations, religious leaders, and the police.

You've probably heard a lot of the things that have been said in this book before. The truth is, it's not very complicated. Even when used correctly, prescription drugs are very powerful and must be respected. It's just plain stupid to abuse them. And swallowing a pill when you are not certain what it is rates as a big-time gamble.

Doctors, pharmacists, drug companies, state and federal agencies, and other groups all have worked hard to make modern medicine safe. We know more about drugs today than we did at any time in our history. Thanks to the efforts of journalists, educators, counselors, and government workers, awareness about prescription drug abuse is increasing. However, the problem can't be entirely solved by doctors, pharmacists, teachers, or the government. It comes down to you.

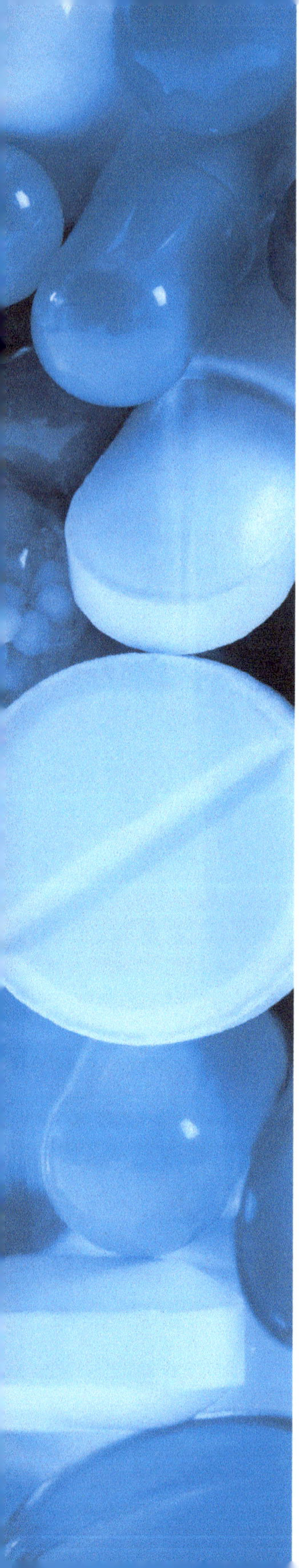

GLOSSARY

addiction A disease characterized by compulsive drug-seeking and abuse of a substance known by the user to be harmful.

amphetamines A group of stimulant drugs that are used to treat certain conditions, such as ADHD, depression, and narcolepsy.

anabolic steroids A group of synthetic hormones related to testosterone that promote tissue growth.

anesthetic A substance that causes loss of sensation or consciousness.

attention deficit/hyperactivity disorder (ADHD) A behavioral disorder that affects attention span, impulse control, and self-discipline. Hyperactivity is a prominent symptom.

barbiturates A group of depressant drugs that are highly addictive. They are used as sedatives, to produce sleep, and to treat epilepsy.

benzodiazepines A group of depressant drugs that are used to treat anxiety and insomnia.

central nervous system The part of the nervous system that includes the brain and spinal cord.

controlled substance A drug or chemical substance whose possession and use are regulated by U.S. law under the Controlled Substances Act.

delirium A mental disturbance characterized by confusion, disordered speech, and hallucinations.

depressant A substance that slows the activity of the central nervous system, reducing anxiety, relieving stress, and producing sleep.

drug abuse Use of a drug in a manner or for a purpose other than that for which it is prescribed.

euphoria An exaggerated feeling of happiness or well-being, especially one that has no basis in reality.

hallucination Something seen or felt that exists only in the mind.

hepatitis Inflammation of the liver, characterized by fever, jaundice, liver enlargement, and weakness.

heroin A powerful illegal drug that is derived from morphine and is a highly addictive narcotic.

hormone A substance produced by one tissue and conveyed by the bloodstream to another to influence processes in the body, such as growth or metabolism.

multiplicative effects Situation in which two or more drugs taken together enhance or multiply the effects of each drug.

narcotics A group of addictive painkilling drugs derived from opium or opium-like compounds. Narcotics can cause drowsiness and significant changes in mood and behavior.

opiate A drug containing or derived from opium and tending to alleviate pain and induce sleep.

opioid A synthetic drug possessing narcotic properties similar to an opiate but not derived from opium.

over-the-counter (OTC) drug A drug legally available for purchase without a doctor's prescription.

pharmacist A person who is licensed to prepare and dispense drugs and medicines.

physical dependence A pattern of substance use in which a person must continue to use a drug to function normally and prevent withdrawal symptoms.

prescription drug A drug used to treat physical and mental health conditions, available legally only with a prescription from a physician.

sedative A drug that produces a calming, quieting, or tranquilizing effect, often given to reduce anxiety or bring on sleep.

seizure A sudden attack, spasm, or convulsion, caused by abnormal electrical activity in the brain.

stimulant A substance that causes increased activity of the nervous or cardiovascular system.

supplement A product taken orally that contains ingredients that are intended to supplement one's diet.

tolerance The capacity of the body to become less responsive to a drug, especially with repeated use. The user then needs more of the drug to get the same effect.

tranquilizer A drug used to reduce mental disturbance, such as anxiety or tension.

unethical Not in accordance with accepted standards of conduct.

withdrawal The act or process of ceasing to use an addictive drug. Symptoms vary from substance to substance.

FOR MORE INFORMATION

Canadian Centre on Substance Abuse (CCSA)
75 Albert Street, Suite 500
Ottawa, ON K1P 5E7
Canada
(613) 235-4048
Web site: http://www.ccsa.ca
For more than twenty years, the CCSA has advanced knowledge and understanding about substance abuse. It provides leadership and research for national initiatives to reduce alcohol- and drug-related harms.

Canadian Foundation for Drug Policy (CFDP)
70 MacDonald Street
Ottawa, ON K2P 1H6
Canada
(613) 236-1027
Web site: http://www.cfdp.ca
The CFDP is a nonprofit organization with a focus on drug policy reform. It serves as a vehicle for discussing drug policy issues with government, the public, other organizations, and the media.

National Institute on Drug Abuse (NIDA)
National Institutes of Health
6001 Executive Boulevard, Room 5213

Bethesda, MD 20892-9561
(301) 443-1124
Web site: http://www.nida.nih.gov
NIDA, a federal agency, brings the power of scientific research to bear on the problems of drug abuse and addiction. The agency's offerings include NIDA for Teens (http://teens.drugabuse.gov), a Web site that offers a wealth of information about prescription drugs and other drug abuse.

Office of National Drug Control Policy (ONDCP)
Drug Policy Information Clearinghouse
P.O. Box 6000
Rockville, MD 20849-6000
(800) 666–3332
Web site: http://www.whitehousedrugpolicy.gov
The ONDCP establishes policies and objectives for the nation's drug control program. Goals include reducing illicit drug use, drug trafficking, and drug-related health consequences.

Substance Abuse and Mental Health Services Administration
1 Choke Cherry Road
Rockville, MD 20857
(877) SAMHSA-7 [726-4727]
Web site: http://www.samhsa.gov
This agency's mission is to reduce the impact of substance abuse and mental illness on America's communities. SAMHSA's Substance Abuse Treatment Facility Locator is a

searchable directory of programs and facilities around the country that treat alcoholism, alcohol abuse, and drug abuse problems.

U.S. Drug Enforcement Administration (DEA)
Office of Diversion Control
8701 Morrissette Drive
Springfield, VA 22152
Web site: http://www.deadiversion.usdoj.gov
The DEA's Office of Diversion Control works to prevent, detect, and investigate the diversion of controlled pharmaceuticals from legitimate sources while ensuring an adequate and uninterrupted supply for legitimate medical, commercial, and scientific needs.

Web Sites

Due to the changing nature of Internet links, Rosen Publishing has developed an online list of Web sites related to the subject of this book. This site is updated regularly. Please use this link to access the list:

http://www.rosenlinks.com/dac/pres

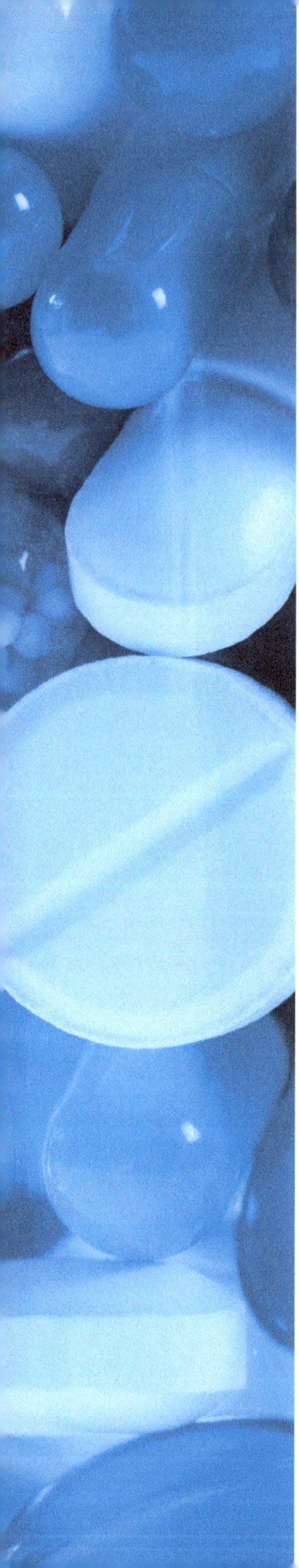

FOR FURTHER READING

Bjornlund, Lydia D. *Prescription Drugs* (Compact Research Series). San Diego, CA: ReferencePoint Press, 2009.

Colvin, Rod. *Overcoming Prescription Drug Addiction: A Guide to Coping and Understanding*. Omaha, NE: Addicus Books, 2008.

Engdahl, Sylvia. *Prescription Drugs* (Current Controversies). Detroit, MI: Greenhaven Press/ Gale Cengage Learning, 2008.

Etingoff, Kim. *Abusing Over-the-Counter Drugs: Illicit Uses for Everyday Drugs* (Illicit and Misused Drugs). Philadelphia, PA: Mason Crest Publishers, 2008.

Klosterman, Lorrie. *The Facts About Depressants* (Drugs). Tarrytown, NY: Marshall Cavendish Benchmark, 2006.

Knowles, Johanna. *Over-the-Counter Drugs* (Junior Drug Awareness). New York, NY: Chelsea House, 2008.

Lynn, Tracy. *Rx*. New York, NY: Simon Pulse, 2006.

Martinez, Jessica. *Virtuosity*. New York, NY: Simon Pulse, 2011.

Nelson, Blake. *Recovery Road*. New York, NY: Scholastic Press, 2011.

Pampel, Fred C. *Prescription Drugs* (Library in a Book). New York, NY: Facts On File, 2010.

Ramen, Fred. *Prescription Drugs* (Drug Abuse and Society). New York, NY: Rosen Publishing, 2007.

Silverman, Harold M. *The Pill Book.* 13th ed. New York, NY: Bantam Books, 2008.

Slade, Suzanne. *OxyContin Abuse* (Incredibly Disgusting Drugs). New York, NY: Rosen Publishing, 2008.

VanVoorst, Jennifer. *Performance-Enhancing Risks: The Science of Steroids* (Headline Science). Mankato, MN: Compass Point Books, 2010.

Walker, Ida. *Painkillers: Prescription Dependency* (Illicit and Misused Drugs). Philadelphia, PA: Mason Crest Publishers, 2008.

West, Krista. *Steroids and Other Performance-Enhancing Drugs* (Junior Drug Awareness). New York, NY: Chelsea House, 2009.

Wolny, Philip. *Abusing Prescription Drugs* (Incredibly Disgusting Drugs). New York, NY: Rosen Publishing, 2008.

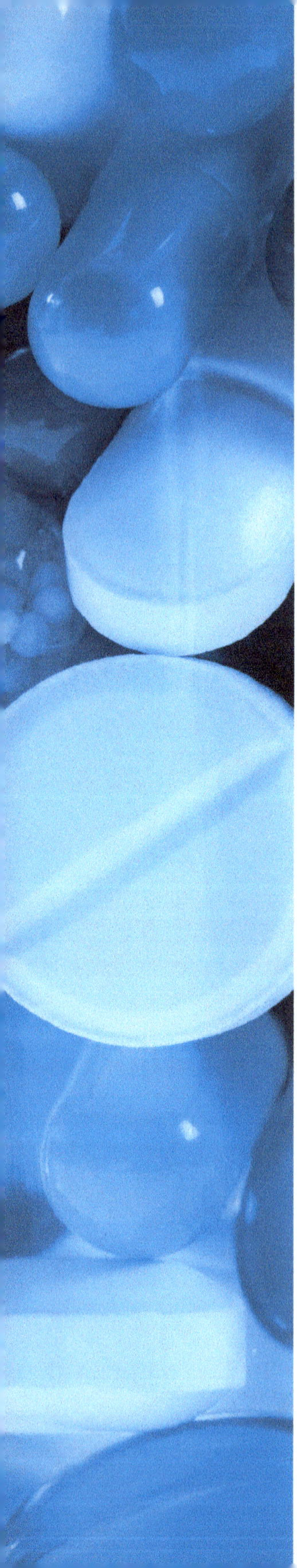

INDEX

About the Authors

Basia Leonard is a health educator and author in New York City.

Jeremy Roberts has written a number of books for young people on various aspects of drug addiction. He lives with his family in upstate New York.

Photo Credits

Cover, p. 1 © www.istockphoto.com/DNY59; pp. 4–5 Comstock Images/Comstock/Thinkstock; pp. 7, 19, 31, 45 Jupiterimages/Polka Dot/Thinkstock; p. 9 Seth Joel/Photodisc/Getty Images; pp. 11, 14–15, 26, 52 Shutterstock; p. 13 Don Farrall/Photodisc/Getty Images; p. 22 Ulrik Tofte/Taxi/Getty Images; pp. 24–25 © Warner Bros./Courtesy Everett Collection; p. 28 Stockbyte/Thinkstock; pp. 34–35 Steve Liss/Time & Life Images/Time & Life Pictures/Getty Images; pp. 38–39 Scott J. Ferell/CQ-Roll Call Group/Congressional Quarterly/Getty Images; pp. 40–41 Darrin Klimek/Digital Vision/Getty Images; p. 42 © Robert W. Ginn/Photo Edit; pp. 46–47 © www.istockphoto.com/selimaksan; p. 51 Will & Demi McIntyre/Photo Researchers.

Editor: Andrea Sclarow; Photo Researcher: Marty Levick